Disc.

An Edward Lear Alphabet

An Edward Lear Alphabet

illustrated by carol newsom

 MULBERRY BOOKS · New York

Library of Congress Cataloging in Publication Data.
Lear, Edward, 1812-1888. An Edward Lear alphabet.
Summary: Illustrations and nonsense verses
introduce the letters of the alphabet. 1. Alphabet
rhymes. 2. Nonsense-verses, English. [1. Alphabet.
2. Nonsense verses. 3. English poetry]
I. Newsom, Carol, ill. II. Title.
PR4879.L2E3   1983   821'.8   82-10037
ISBN 0-688-00965-4 (lib. bdg.)

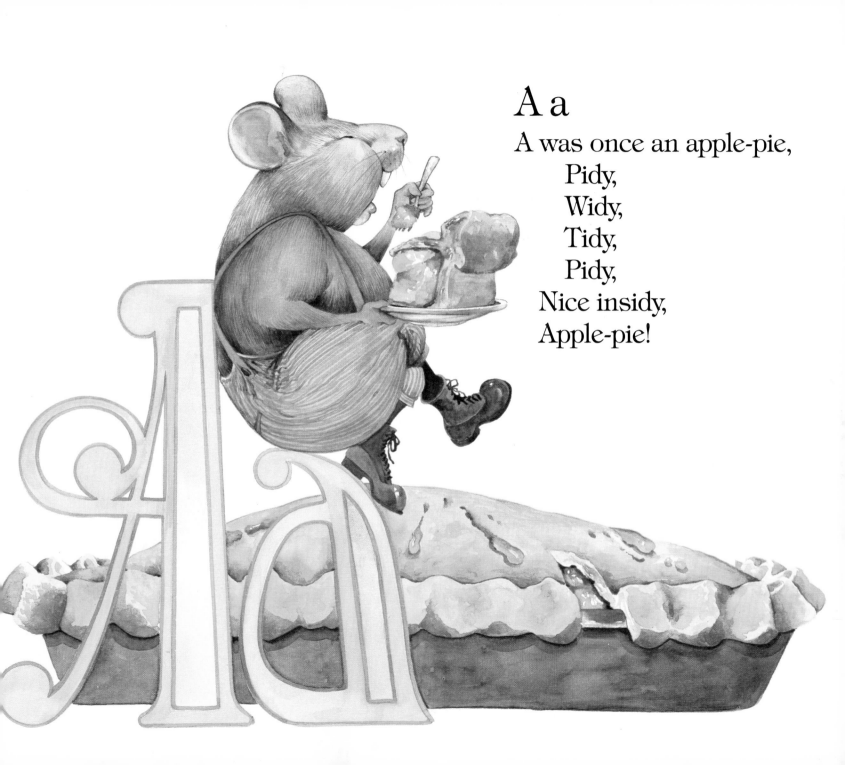

A a

A was once an apple-pie,
  Pidy,
  Widy,
  Tidy,
  Pidy,
  Nice insidy,
  Apple-pie!

B b
B was once a little bear,
   Beary,
   Wary,
   Hairy,
   Beary,
   Taky cary,
   Little bear!

C c

C was once a little cake,
 Caky,
 Baky,
 Maky,
 Caky,
 Taky Caky,
 Little cake!

D d

D was once a little doll,
    Dolly,
    Molly,
    Polly,
    Nolly,
    Nursy dolly,
    Little doll!

E e
E was once a little eel,
    Eely,
    Weely,
    Peely,
    Eely,
Twirly, tweely,
Little eel!

F f
F was once a little fish,
Fishy,
Wishy,
Squishy,
Fishy,
In a dishy,
Little fish!

G g
G was once a little goose,
    Goosy,
    Moosy,
    Boosey,
    Goosey,
    Waddly-woosy,
Little goose!

H h
H was once a little hen,
    Henny,
    Chenny,
    Tenny,
    Henny,
    Eggsy-any,
    Little hen?

I i

I was once a bottle of ink,
    Inky,
    Dinky,
    Thinky,
    Inky,
    Blacky minky,
    Bottle of ink!

J j

J was once a jar of jam,
Jammy,
Mammy,
Clammy,
Jammy,
Sweety, swammy,
Jar of jam!

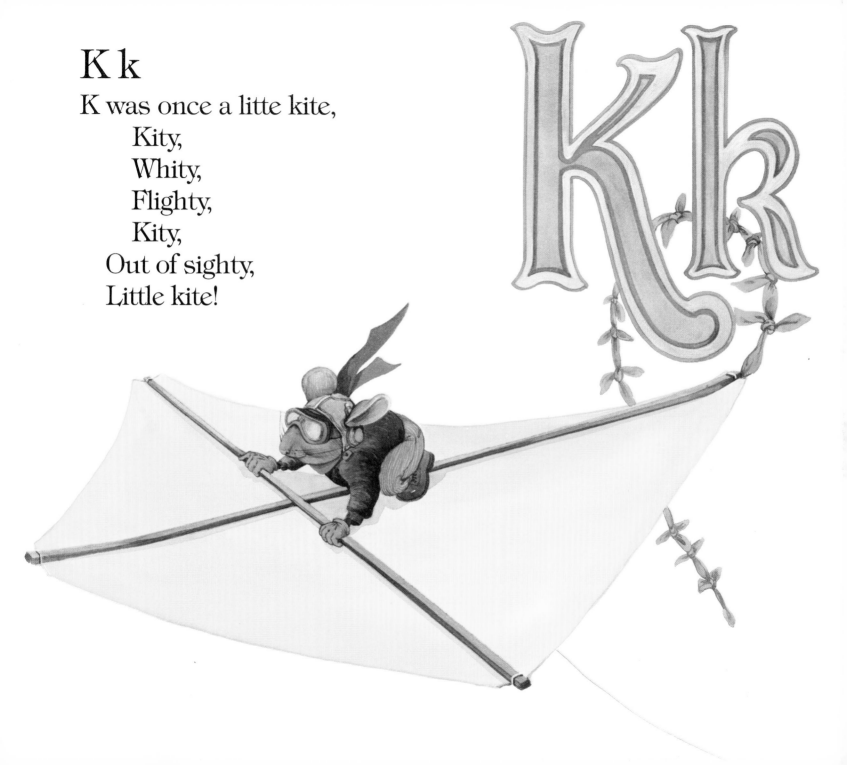

K k
K was once a litte kite,
    Kity,
    Whity,
    Flighty,
    Kity,
    Out of sighty,
    Little kite!

L 1

L was once a little lark,
 Larky,
 Marky,
 Harky,
 Larky,
 In the parky,
 Little lark!

M m
M was once a little mouse,
 Mousy,
 Bousy,
 Sousy,
 Mousy,
 In the housy,
 Little mouse!

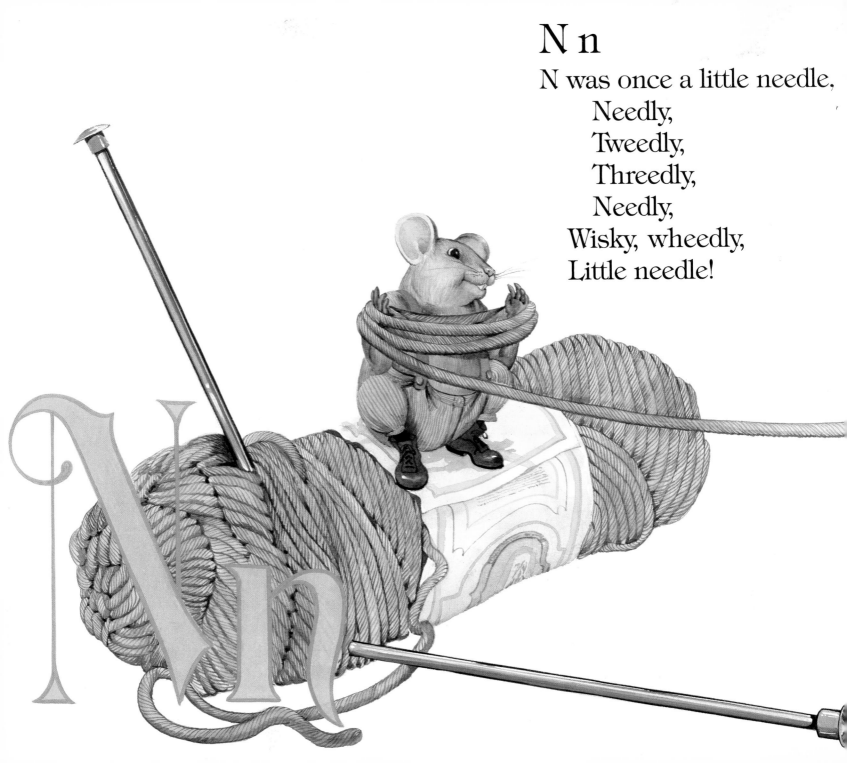

N n
N was once a little needle,
    Needly,
    Tweedly,
    Threedly,
    Needly,
    Wisky, wheedly,
Little needle!

O o

was once a little owl,
    Owly,
    Prowly,
    Howly,
    Owly,
Browny fowly,
Little owl!

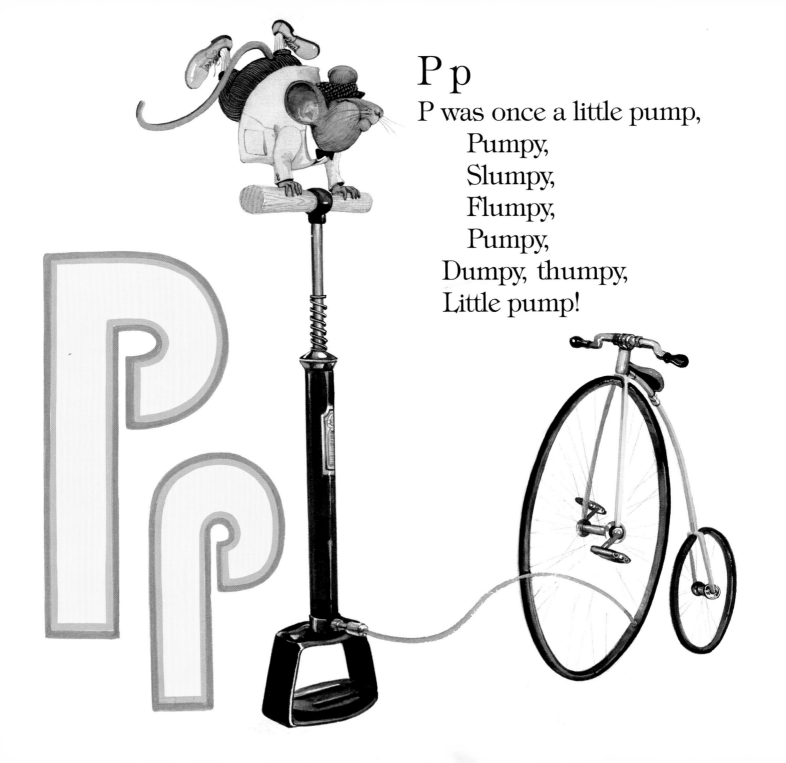

P p
P was once a little pump,
    Pumpy,
    Slumpy,
    Flumpy,
    Pumpy,
    Dumpy, thumpy,
    Little pump!

Q q

Q was once a little quail,
Quaily,
Faily,
Daily,
Quaily,
Stumpy-taily,
Little quail!

R r

R was once a little rose,
    Rosy,
    Posy,
    Nosy,
    Rosy,
Blows-y, grows-y,
Little rose!

S s

S was once a little shrimp,
    Shrimpy,
    Nimpy,
    Flimpy,
    Shrimpy,
    Jumpy, jimpy,
    Little shrimp!

T t

T was once a little thrush,
    Thrushy,
    Hushy,
    Bushy,
    Thrushy,
    Flitty, flushy,
Little thrush!

U u

U was once a little urn,
   Urny,
   Burny,
   Turny,
   Urny,
   Bubbly, burny,
Little urn!

V v
V was once a little vine,
    Viny,
    Winy,
    Twiny,
    Viny,
    Twisty-twiny,
    Little vine!

W w

W was once a whale,
　　　Whaly,
　　　Scaly,
　　　Shaly,
　　　Whaly,
　　　Tumbly-taily,
　　　Mighty whale!

X x

X was once a great king Xerxes,
  Xerxy,
  Perxy,
  Turxy,
  Xerxy,
Linxy, lurxy,
Great King Xerxes!

Y y

Y was once a little yew,
    Yewdy,
    Fewdy,
    Crudy,
    Yewdy,
Growdy, grewdy,
Little yew!

Z z
Z was once a piece of zinc,
    Tinky,
    Winky,
    Blinky,
    Tinky,
    Tinky minky,
    Piece of zinc!

EDWARD LEAR was born at Highgate near London on May 12, 1812, the twentieth child in a family of twenty-one children. He began earning his living by drawing at the age of fifteen. When he was nineteen he was employed by the Zoological Society of London to do animal drawings. His illustrations of birds for zoologist John Gould of the British Museum were highly praised and ranked with those of Audubon. Because of poor health, from age twenty-five on he visited England regularly, but spent most of his time traveling in the warm climates of Italy, Greece, Egypt, and the Middle East. He published seven books about his travels, which he illustrated with landscapes. In 1846 he tutored Queen Victoria in drawing and, in the same year, published his first *Book of Nonsense*, which was written for the children of the 13th earl of Derby under the pseudonym Derry down Derry. The book was an instant success, and he soon became best known as a humorist. He eventually settled in San Remo, Italy, where he produced several volumes of humorous nonsense rhymes, limericks, and alphabets, one of which was "A was once an apple-pie." Despite failing eyesight and poor health, he kept at his writing until his death at San Remo, January 29, 1888.